# *LOVE IS...A ROSE*

by

Pamela S. Thibodeaux

***Presented To:***

_____

***From:***

_____

***Date:***

_____

***Inscription:***

_____

_____

_____

_____

_____

_____

_____

# *LOVE IS...A ROSE*

by

Pamela S. Thibodeaux

*Love is a Rose*
By: Pamela S. Thibodeaux
Copyright © 2013

**Publisher/Distributor:**
Temperance Publishing, an imprint of
Pamela S Thibodeaux Enterprises, LLC
PO Box 324; Iowa, LA 70647

**ISBN#:** 978-0-9896728-1-8

**Cover Design:** Delia Latham (Delia's Designs)

**THE ROSE (1014412)**
Words and Music by Amanda McBroom
© 1977 (Renewed) WARNER-TAMERLANE
PUBLISHING CORP. and THIRD STORY MUSIC,
INC. All Rights Administered by WARNER-
TAMERLANE PUBLISHING CORP. All Rights
Reserved

*\*Used by Permission of ALFRED
PUBLISHING CO., INC. ~ License #
PR130614-2002*

Note:

This is a work of personal, creative nonfiction. No part of this publication may be reproduced, stored in or introduced into a retrieval system, or transmitted, in any form, or by means (electronic, mechanical, photocopying, recording, or other-wise), without the prior written permission of the above publisher of this book. The scanning, uploading, and distribution of this book via the Internet or via any other means without the permission of the publisher is illegal and punishable by law. Please purchase only authorized electronic editions, and do not participate in or encourage electronic piracy of copyrighted materials. Your support of the author's rights is appreciated.

## *Praise for Love is a Rose*

*"Pam Thibodeaux writes a beautiful and heart felt devotional in Love is a Rose. She has personally walked the valleys of sorrow and suffering and God has used her journey to reach into our hearts and lives with some deep and thought provoking questions. I highly endorse this book."* Rita A Schulte, LPC. http://ritaschulte.com/

*"Through Pamela's blessed ability to find God everywhere, even in secular song lyrics, she has written devotions guaranteed to touch the heart and remind the reader of our True Love, the Rose of Sharon."* Linday Yezak, Author, Editor Triple Edge Critique Service

*"'If love is like a river then the only reed it should drown is one of prejudice, fear or hate. Rivers of love should buoy a tender reed"* **and** *"Seeds to ponder: If God will not break, crush or even spurn a bruised reed, why then do we insist on ripping apart one another's hearts, minds, lives, and spirits in word or deed?' are two examples of the powerful words written by*

*Pamela Thibodeaux. Using the lyrics of the song, "The Rose", she creatively and skillfully breathes a fresh perspective of the word of God to show her readers that God does indeed speak in unsuspecting ways. Love is a Rose, is guaranteed to soften every heart and reveal God's love in a way that is tangible, desirable, and life-changing. I whole-heartedly recommend it. I am forever-changed and have been reminded to listen for God's voice in unusual places."* Teresa Ortiz, Author & Publishing Director, Stonebridge Publications
http://stonebridgepublications.com

*"Love is a Rose is the proof modern believers need that what was written over two thousand years ago is still relevant in 2013. Author Pamela Thibodeaux gently peels away the layers of humanity and teaches the message of grace and mercy in her inspirational devotional. Does God go beyond the church walls to woo his beloved? You bet! Even through contemporary music. Especially through contemporary music."* Mary Nichelson, Member EPA-Evangelical Press Association
http://www.marysworld411.com

*Praise for Pamela S Thibodeaux*

*"Thibodeaux leads the reader through from the first page to the last without once relinquishing control. She hooks them, holds them, and keeps them enthralled until the last line."* ~ Review of **The Visionary** by Delia Latham.

*"**In His Sight** caught my attention from the beginning and it made me wonder if I had given all to God as he gave all to me. Thank you, Pamela for a story that I would readily recommend to anyone who needs that extra encouragement!"* ~ Reviewed by Wendy for Happily Ever After Reviews.

*"**Winter Madness** is a wonderful romance and an excellent example of spiritual growth."* ~Reviewed by Dee Daily for The Romance Studio.

*"**A Hero for Jessica** is a good, sweet read charged with attraction but an emphasis on true love. I recommend it to women of all ages."* ~ Reviewed by Violet for LASR.

"***Cathy's Angel*** *is a short tale that is entertaining as well as inspiring. Well done!"* ~ Reviewed by Marlene for Fallen Angel Reviews.

*"Pamela S. Thibodeaux's motto is "Inspirational with an Edge!" Her short story **Choices** lives up to those words and is well worth reading."* ~Reviewed by Gail for Night Owl Romance.

*"**The Inheritance** was my first Thibodeaux work; however, it will not be my last! Her approach to writing about everyday life, while struggling to maintain strict Christian standards and values, is a glimpse into reality which we all must face from time to time."* ~ Reviewed by Brenda Talley for The Romance Studio.

*"If you have ever considered Christian fiction bland, then check out the **Tempered Series**. It will be well worth your time."* ~ Amanda Killgore ~ for Huntress Reviews.

*"**Lori's Redemption** is fast paced, lots of action, gripping storyline.... I loved it. It's gone straight back into my TBR pile."* ~ Clare Revell author of "Monday's Child" series.

## *Dedication*

The writing herein came by divine inspiration so that you, the reader, will know the reality, the simplicity, and the necessity of a personal relationship with God through our Lord and Savior, Jesus Christ. To HE Who is the Rose of Sharon, be all the glory.

Love is a Rose

## *Introduction*

The Bible talks of harps playing and choirs of angelic hosts singing. It also tells us to "make a joyful noise unto the Lord." The Israelites were ordered to send the praise and worship team—playing musical instruments, dancing and singing—ahead of the soldiers into battle. So there must be something special and powerful about music.

Music is an intricate element of worship, an aspect of praise that brings you into intimate proximity with the Lord. Music lifts you physically (fatigue disappears, pain is forgotten), mentally (your mind is filled with it, erasing everything else), emotionally (you are saturated with joy and peace) and spiritually (your spirit soars on the wings of His); opening your heart and mind to receive more of God's presence, more of His truth.

Music is the magical entry into the spirit world; the golden gate into the Kingdom of God. But we mustn't be of the mindset that God only uses Christian music to reach out and touch our mind, heart and spirit. God uses any and every means available to speak to His children.

Our job is to be open and receptive.

Nearly every Christian song I hear touches my heart in some way, urging me into a closer walk with God and bringing me a truer knowledge of Jesus. Amazingly though, the one song that really opened my spirit to a deeper understanding of the abundance of His grace and mercy wasn't a Christian song but a Country one.

I'll never forget the morning in 1995 when The Rose as performed by Conway Twitty came to me in its entirety with Bible references or Scriptures correlating to every verse....

**Some say love, it is a river that drowns the tender reed...** *"A bruised reed He will not break."*

**Some say love, it is a razor that leaves your soul to bleed....**Bible Conversion; a cutting or stripping away of old beliefs.

**Some say love, it is a hunger, an endless, aching need...** *"As the hind* *longs for running water, so my soul longs for thee oh God..."*

**I say love, it is a flower, and you its only seed...** *"If you have faith the size of a mustard seed..."*

**It's the heart, afraid of breaking, that never learns to dance...** David danced before the Lord.

**It's the dream, afraid of waking, that never takes the chance...** *"Entrust your works unto the Lord and your plans will succeed."*

**It's the one who won't be taken, who cannot seem to give...** *"Love is not selfish...For God so loved the world He GAVE...!"*

**And the soul, afraid of dying, that never learns to live...** *"What shall a man give in exchange for his soul? For what is man profited if he should gain the whole world but lose his soul?"* Or more accurately...*"Let not your heart be anxious, for I am with you always, even unto the end of time."*

**When the night has been too lonely, and the road has been too**

**long...** "*I am going but I will not leave you alone. I will send you a comforter, a counselor to guide and help you.*"

**And you think that love is only for the lucky and the strong....** *"God is love and he who dwells in love dwells with God. The meek shall inherit the earth...blessed are the poor in spirit, for theirs is the kingdom of God."*

**Just remember in the winter** (of darkness and sin)....Jesus died so that we might have life, He conquered sin and darkness.... *"I came so that you might have life, in abundance, to the full, overflowing."*

**Far beneath the bitter snows...** How can something so beautiful, so pure, be so bitter and cold? God is light. He washes us clean with the shed blood of His Son so that we might be as pure as the snow.

**Lies the seed**, (of faith**)... that with the sun's** (Son's) **love... in the spring**... (season of new birth, new life)... **becomes the rose** (an attractive flower).

### *Wow, what a revelation!*

I immediately sat down and wrote the ensuing compilation paralleling the love of

God and the life of a Christian to the words of this song.

Why do you suppose God used a country song to teach me about Himself?

I believe God was using a means familiar to me to show the depth and power of His love for me.

It is my prayer the words contained herein will do the same for you.

Before I begin, let me answer a few questions about myself. I am not a minister or even a candidate for the ministry. I have no degree or doctorate in psychology or anything resembling either. I am simply a Christian housewife and mother who's been blessed with a talent for writing and who desires to glorify the Lord of my life with that talent.

As I said in my opening statement, the Lord led me to write this analogy so the words in it (and I'm sure He also led the songwriter to write such a beautiful song) are His, guided through me by the power of the Holy Spirit to speak to you.

I have included pages for reflection. Please use them as you see fit to record your thoughts and what you feel God is speaking to you through this devotional.

Now, let's begin.

### *Reflection*

Love is a Rose

## *Reflection*

## *Reflection*

Love is a Rose

## *What Is Love?*

The Bible tells us that love is:

**Long-suffering**: Love is patient, kind, and understanding. It is not boastful or jealous and it bears all things and never fails. 1 Cor. 13:4-5

**Omnipotent:** God is omnipotent. The definition of omnipotent is "infinite and unlimited power." God is these things and God is Love.

**Visual:** In the beauty around us and in the vision of Heaven. We are told that "eyes have not seen" what God has prepared for those who love Him. We get a glimpse of the promise when we look for the beauty in the world around us.

**Everlasting:** Jesus said, "I have loved you with an everlasting love," and "He who believes in me shall never die, but have life everlasting."

We see that Love is good.

## Thibodeaux

### *Reflection*

Love is a Rose

## *What is a Rose?*

The dictionary describes the rose as "an attractive flower" it also defines rosary as: *"A sequence of prayers; a rose garden."* So we see that the rose is a symbol of grace and beauty.

We all love to share roses with loved ones. Their beauty has been symbolic of love for generations and appreciated to this day. The Bible talks of the Rose of Sharon and the Rose of Jericho. Now we see that a rose garden symbolizes the rosary.

Catholics know very much the power of the rosary and the power of a novena to St. Theresa. You may wonder what this particular novena to this particular Saint has to do with this analogy.

The reason is this: A rose is the sign from St. Theresa that answered prayer is near.

Of course we all know that only God has the power to answer prayer, but the intercession of a Saint is firmly believed and established in the Catholic faith. Many who are led by the Holy Spirit feel that one does not have to be "Catholic" to believe in the power of intercessory prayer by a Saint. You only need faith and you must pray that your prayer be granted according to the Holy will of the Father. Even a Saint cannot change His mind and God will not grant you something that is outside His will for you.

There are numerous testimonies to the power of a novena to St. Theresa (and many other Saints). Stories of roses appearing on pizza boxes, or drawn and colored by a child and given to the person praying or of silk roses found on the side of the road in "the middle of nowhere," and petitions being granted are simple ways in which prayers to this beloved Saint helped bring peace in a stressful situation. Guidepost magazine printed an article where a woman was sending roses to her mother and gave one to a woman whom she'd seen on several occasions and "appeared to be down." The giver later found out that the rose symbolized the answer to the recipient's prayers!

Catholics are not the only faith denomination to believe in the symbolism of roses. Some of the old religious beliefs in the African American culture state when an

# Love is a Rose

elderly or ill person dreams of a rose garden it is an indication that death and Heaven is near.

Now that we've established the link between love and roses and their purpose in faith, let's continue with our analogy.

## *Reflection*

_____

_____

_____

_____

_____

_____

_____

_____

_____

_____

## *Reflection*

Love is a Rose

***Some say love, it is a river that drowns the tender reed...***

The Bible talks about "rivers of living water."

Jesus said, "He who comes to me will never thirst."

We have a song that claims "love is like a river flowing out into the desert for you and me."

If Love is like a river then the only reed it should drown is one of prejudice, fear or hate. Rivers of love should buoy a tender reed.

Isaiah 42:3 and Matthew 12:20 say, "A bruised reed He will not break."

God calls us into the river of His love. We are renewed by His Spirit, cleansed in the waters of baptism and purified by the Blood of Christ; the blood that flowed from his side mixed with water.

Where I live in Louisiana it is easy to observe water and its many characteristics. The gentle lap of waves against the bottom of a boat, the crash of the tide rolling in along the Gulf shore, or the roar of a tidal surge as it sweeps away everything in its path.

Many times we feel like we're drowning in our circumstances. Bills are piled up, family is in turmoil, and stress is our daily diet. What do we do? To whom or what do we turn for even a moment's peace? Let us turn to the Christ within who is the Prince of Peace and let us offer that peace to our fellow man in the spirit of love and forgiveness. By sharing peace, you not only teach peace but cultivate a peaceful lifestyle.

***Seeds to ponder:*** If God will not break, crush or even spurn a bruised reed, why then do we insist on ripping apart one another's hearts, minds, lives, and spirits in word or deed?

**Prayer**: Dear Lord, show me the tender reeds I have crushed with my insensitivity. Please forgive me—help me to make amends with this person if only within my own heart and mind.

Love is a Rose

## *Reflection*

Thibodeaux

## *Reflection*

## Love is a Rose

***Some say love, it is a razor that leaves your soul to bleed...***

This is perhaps one of the more difficult lines of the song to relate and compare to the love of God and the life of a Christian. The Bible talks about a conversion. It lists the conversions of many and refers to a conversion as a "cutting or stripping away of old beliefs."

The dictionary defines a conversion as a "change in beliefs."

In John 15: 2, Jesus said about the Father, "Every branch that bears fruit He prunes, that it may bear more fruit."

So we could say God's love is like a razor or rather, a pruning tool. He cuts out the bad and strips away old beliefs. As a gardener would prepare rose bushes, He prepares the heart for truth, which leads to life and beauty.

As for leaving the soul to bleed, Christ bled for us on the cross at Calvary. Our soul may not bleed literally, but whenever we hurt for someone or over an injustice to the innocent, our heart and soul "bleeds" for them. Every time we pray for the needs of others that prayer is likened to little drops of blood into the heart of the Father. It moistens, fertilizes and brings new life to the faith of the believer. There is no greater prayer than that of a believer on someone else's behalf.

On the other hand, every time we hurt someone—whether physically, mentally or emotionally, we may as well cut their heart out and leave their soul wide open and bleeding all over the place.

There was a time I let someone whom I considered a friend rent my house. This was not just rental property, this was my home—the place I'd shared with my husband of twenty years. He'd passed away and I was unable to withstand the pain of living there without him so this seemed like the perfect solution. Someone I loved and trusted would be there to take care of my precious memories. Unfortunately this is not how it turned out. By the time she moved out the vinyl flooring was torn beyond repair, the walls were painted an atrocious hodgepodge of colors and appliances didn't work as they did when she moved in. The damage to my property was mild in comparison to the devastation of my heart. She desecrated my home! Oh, it wasn't the house itself—I couldn't live there and didn't want the house anyway. The fact that she betrayed my trust is what hurt most.

Houses can be repaired; hearts take a little longer to heal.

Even as I write this many months later, the ache chafes and I realize healing isn't complete. I also know the best way to get to a place of true peace and healing is through forgiveness. So I pray... "I forgive you and I release you to God," and trust the blood of Jesus to do the restorative work in my heart and soul.

***Seeds to ponder:*** Cruelty and insensitivity have no place in the life of a Christian and yet, we are all guilty and fall short of the glory of God in so many ways when it comes to our relationships. Let us take care and not leave any soul to bleed.

**Prayer:** Dearest Lord, please show me the ways in which I hurt others, especially those unintentional or careless words that cut deeper than any knife could—help me to be more sensitive to Your Spirit before I speak or act in a manner unworthy of Your child.

## *Reflection*

_____

_____

_____

_____

_____

_____

_____

_____

_____

_____

_____

_____

_____

## Love is a Rose

***Some say love, it is a hunger, an endless aching need...***

How very true! The Bible speaks of a longing of our soul to be in communion with the Lord. Psalm 42 says, "As the hind longs for running water, so my soul longs for thee, oh God..."

Endless, aching need; we all feel it—— the need to be loved, to be worthy; the ache to know God more intimately and to glorify Him.

Many describe this aspect of their walk with God as an ache or a hunger which is forever present. Sometimes it is more prevalent than others but always there....The need to be close to Him, to know His will, to feel His presence, to be made worthy and whole by His Holy Spirit.

Just when we feel we've gotten closer to Him still, the ache smarts again——deeper, more desperate than the last time. A longing that cannot be described——one that can only be satisfied by the Holy Spirit leading you closer and deeper into the Sacred Heart of Jesus.

Every one of us can relate to the insatiable hunger we've experienced in our lives. Many times we seek after and pursue more...bigger and better things (money, houses, cars, jobs) thinking those will satisfy, not realizing the hunger in our soul is one only God can satisfy. As I look back over my life, I recall a time when I got wrapped up in the things of the world, and yet, I've always been a seeker of peace above all things. Oh, that we would teach our children that more is not better and the more things you have, the more time you'll spend taking care of them and the less time you'll have to pursue what really matters in life—people and relationships!

The accumulation of things will never satisfy the soul like an intimate relationship with the Creator and His creation. Get rid of the "stuff" in your life and see how much peace there is in simplicity.

***Seeds to ponder:*** In Matthew 5: 6, Jesus said, "Blessed are those who hunger and thirst for righteousness, for they shall be filled." How many times do we fill the hunger in our hearts with things of the

# Love is a Rose

world instead of filling it with things of the Spirit?

**Prayer:** Dear God, help me to recognize true, spiritual hunger and turn to You instead of giving in to the lusts of my flesh and the lure of the world by engaging in unholy attitudes and actions.

## *Reflection*

_____

_____

_____

_____

_____

_____

_____

_____

_____

_____

## *Reflection*

Love is a Rose

***I say love, it is a flower, and you its only seed...***

Faith is a seed that blossoms into flowers of hope and joy. The Bible says that, "God's word will not come back void."

We are told to plant seeds of faith, water them with prayer, fertilize them with hope and watch with joy as they blossom into flowers of blessing.

**Matthew 17:20** tells us that if we have faith as a mustard seed we can move mountains.

**Galatians 3:29** says that if we are Christ's, then we are Abraham's seed, and heirs according to the promise.

Therefore, no prayer goes unheard or unanswered. What we must realize is that God's answer may not always be what we think it should be.

When we get intimate with the Lord and learn His ways, we'll see our seeds of faith blossom and grow into rose gardens of blessings because when we're intimate with

Him and know His ways, our prayers will be in alignment with His will for our lives.

God is happy to grant our prayers and bless our lives if we *"ask in faith and believe that you receive."* But remember God will give *"good things to those who ask"* He will not grant you something you think would be a blessing but would ultimately be for your ruin!

Some wise soul once said, *"Sometimes God withholds our answer until we have gained the knowledge, acquired the wisdom, or formed the character to appreciate what He has chosen to bless us with."*

Think about it! Would you rather get what you "want" or what He wants for you?

Knowing God as the generous, loving, Father He is, it is more prudent to have what He gives because only He knows what's best for us, and when we understand this our lives will be simpler and much more peaceful.

Many of us have a dream of where we'll go and what we'll do when we get the perfect job, retire, or hit the big jackpot, thinking life will be better "once I get there." God calls us to "bloom where we're planted." Believing something else, or someone new, or some other place will make us happy, will only lead to discontent.

Happiness comes from within and one of the quickest ways to true bliss is to get over yourself and sow joy and happiness into someone else's life! This is such a simple thing...a phone call, email, note, letter or card. Even a simple smile can brighten someone's day. Make sharing love, peace and joy a priority in your life and watch dreams become reality and miracles happen.

***Seeds to ponder:*** God is love. If love is a flower, and you its only seed—how can you plant seeds of love and faith into the lives of others?

**Prayer:** Dear Lord, You said, "Assuredly, I say to you, inasmuch as you did it to one of the least of these My brethren, you did it to Me" AND "Inasmuch as you did not do it to one of the least of these, you did not do it to Me." Please help me to see the good I do and that which I don't and to strive in all things to show Your love, mercy and grace unto the least of my brethren.

### *Reflection*

Love is a Rose

***It's the heart afraid of breaking that never learns to dance...***

Scripture tells us that David danced before the Lord. If you're too afraid to dance you'll never really appreciate the music or experience the joy of living. No one said it would be easy, even Jesus said, *"Take up your cross daily."*

Oh, but the joy! As you become stronger in your faith and closer to Him, you will know such joy.

This verse is also reflective of those who won't open their hearts to love because they are afraid of being hurt. Love is a gift and we should embrace it with our entire being. True...it may not last and you may be hurt, but as Tennyson said, *"It is better to have loved and lost than never to have loved at all."*

I love to go out dancing. Nothing soothes my soul, energizes my spirit or relieves my stress more than good music and a sawdust covered floor. Many judge Christians like me who enjoy a night out on the town but we must be careful not to do so. As Jesus said, *"Man looks on the appearance but God knows the heart."*

So love, dance!

Participate in the dance of life. Sing to the Lord a new song. Express your faith. Step out into the deep waters of trust. You can walk on them. You may stumble, you may even fall—but remember, it is at those times, the times when you stumble and fall, that He carries you. Remember, it is "by your weakness that God is made strong."

***Seeds to Ponder***: So many shun dancing as immoral or evil and many condemn those who sway and dance in the isle of their church, but the Bible is full of instances where people danced in honor of the Lord. How can we judge someone for dancing when we don't know the condition of their heart?

**Prayer:** Dear Lord, help me to get over myself—my shyness or insecurity—and dance before You when I feel Your Spirit welling up within me and help me to suspend my judgment on those who aren't afraid to do so.

Love is a Rose

*Reflection*

## *Reflection*

Love is a Rose

***It's the dream, afraid of waking, that never takes a chance...***

We all have dreams. The Bible says that He shall "give you the desires of your heart." It also tells us to "entrust your works unto the Lord and your plans will succeed."

Though He gives us dreams, talents and gifts (and it says so in Corinthians) we must use them for His glory!

From the time I could articulate, my biggest dream was to be married and have a family. I often say having a marriage where bliss was the norm out of which came four loving and responsible children is my greatest accomplishments. One day while talking with my Pastor after my husband's death, I reiterated this story to him and told of my frustration of not knowing if God had a different plan and purpose for my life now that that dream had ended. His response was, "God's plan for you hasn't changed," and I realized the dream to be a wife was one He had placed in my heart from the time I was a little girl playing with baby dolls. A desire that grew and flourished through those years of adolescence where I spent hours reading romance novels and planning for my Prince Charming. God did not create us to go through life alone and a happy marriage is a joy to Him and a blessing onto the world.

Although my husband's demise has left a huge hole in my heart, my desire to be a wife is still there, buried beneath the grief, and I know one day I'll be whole enough to welcome a new love into my life.

What is the biggest dream, the deepest desire of your heart? Keep dreaming! Make plans! But, stay in touch with Him to bring it to pass in His perfect timing. "Entrust your works (dreams, plans, and goals) unto the Lord and they will succeed."

***Seeds to ponder:*** Some of the greatest spiritual teachers of our time exhort the power of the imagination, dreams and visualization. The book of Joel tells us that God will pour out His Spirit and that old men shall dream, young men shall see visions and daughters shall prophesy. Have you ever considered that the biggest dream in your heart has been placed there by God?

## Love is a Rose

That this desire is what He desires for you and designed to bless the world as part of His plan?

**Prayer:** Heavenly Father, show me the dreams You have placed in my heart and the pathways by which to accomplish them for Your glory and a blessing onto the world to make this a better place for all of mankind.

### *Reflection*

_____

_____

_____

_____

_____

_____

_____

_____

_____

## *Reflection*

Love is a Rose

***It's the one, who won't be taken, who cannot seem to give...***

This is another difficult verse to relate to. There aren't many who "won't take" but numerous who "cannot seem to give." It's usually take and take and give little or nothing in return. Remember: Love is not jealous, inflated or rude and does not seek after its own interests." The definition of selfish is "caring only for oneself." It should not be this way with the Christian!

We are called to give. The Bible says "give and it shall be given unto you; good measure, pressed down, shaken together and running over." We cannot expect the Lord to bless us if we give nothing of ourselves in return. Most people look at this scripture in terms of money or material wealth. I'm telling you it means give in everything. If you give "freely and cheerfully," it'll be given back and multiplied "freely and cheerfully."

God loves a cheerful giver. You must give of your time, money, talent, energy, everything. God sees and blesses in return.

How many times have you heard "you can't out give God"?

This is especially true in the area of forgiveness and perhaps the most difficult commandment in the life of a Christian.

Oh, it's easy to say; "I forgive." But, oh, so hard to mean it; Jesus forgave from the cross. How much more should we forgive? He taught us to pray, "Forgive us our trespasses as we forgive those who trespass against us." He warned us not to come to the Father with malice or unforgiveness in our hearts.

Again, this is perhaps one of the more difficult areas of giving in the life of a Christian. We don't always forget even though we feel we've forgiven. Regarding our sins, Isaiah 43 says that God "remembers them not." Shouldn't we do the same?

There are many books on this subject and it can sometimes take years of forgiving that one person or incident before you are healed of the painful memories. Sometimes you must do it daily. Pray for the grace to forgive and accept His grace, mercy and forgiveness for yourself. Pray and believe: "I forgive and accept forgiveness for..." Also, pray for the grace to make the forgiveness real. Forgiveness is a conscious act of our will. Only God's grace can make the forgiveness we choose to extend a true emotion.

Speaking from experience: It works. The pain lessens when you realize that you have forgiven this person (even if it's yourself) and you must accept forgiveness for your part or for your un-forgiveness. This gets even easier when you realize it is Satan who constantly reminds you of the injury or guilt linked to unforgiveness.

Scripture tells us that God places our transgressions "as far as the east is from the west" from His mind. So, when you are reminded (by the devil) of your unforgiveness, close your eyes and pray "in the name of Jesus I have forgiven and accept forgiveness and I release my anger, resentment and hurt."

And, when you think it's taking a long time for healing and you are not loved or worthy, and you're tired of being the one to always give. remember this: For God so loved the world that he GAVE...

I'll never forget my biggest lesson in forgiveness. I was writing my novel, Tempered Dreams, which deals with domestic violence. While working on an an intense scene where the heroine's mother dies from a beating, the Lord spoke to my heart. "Dedicate the book to your ex-husband in the spirit of forgiveness." What?!? Are You serious, Lord? You want me to put in writing for the entire world to see that I lived in an abusive relationship?

Regardless of how many arguments I came up with, I knew what He had spoken to my spirit. "Okay, Lord let me finish the book then we'll talk about it," I promised, but I knew there would be no talking. When God speaks, He is not open for discussion, only obedience. So I finished the book and wrote the dedication. Not only did God hammer home the necessity of forgiveness to me, but to my heroine, and numerous readers as well.

***Seeds to Ponder:*** A Course in Miracles says "forgiveness is the key to happiness." What resentments do you hold in your heart? Who have you not forgiven? Mark Twain said "forgiveness is the fragrance the flower leaves on the heel that crushes it." One of the most powerful prayers you can utter is, "I forgive you and I release you to God."

Try it; it works miracles in your heart, your mind, and your life!

**Prayer:** Father God, I know forgiveness is the key to happiness, mine and for those whom I've withheld forgiveness. Show me how to let go of my thoughts and feelings of anger and resentment and to love my enemies as You have loved me. Help me to let go and let Your love and peace produce a beautiful fragrance where once anger was a stench in Your nostrils.

## *Reflection*

_____

_____

_____

_____

_____

## *Reflection*

Love is a Rose

***And the soul, afraid of dying, that never learns to live...***

The dictionary defines the soul as "the Spiritual part of humans; the essential element." Matthew 16:26 says, "For what is man profited if he should gain the whole world but lose his soul?" Or "What shall a man give in exchange for his soul?" The body cannot live without the soul, but the soul can live, eternally, without the body. But only through Jesus!

Twyla Paris sings a song that says, "You are the Risen King, that you would come and fill my soul is beyond a dream." Though it is beyond a dream, it can be a reality. For it is a truth. When we invite Jesus into our hearts, He fills our soul and dwells within our body. Remember, the Bible says, "You are the temple of the Lord."

The longing of the soul can only be fulfilled with Christ. We may try and satisfy that longing with drugs, alcohol, sex, material possessions or any number of things, but what we truly need and long for is communion with Jesus. The Christ. The Lord. The Risen King. The soul cannot live without Him. Nor without faith or hope. For He is our hope and our faith is in Him. As is our joy.

How much and in how many ways do we fear death and dying? Sometimes so much that we miss out on living. We can't "not live," but we can live a life substandard of God's best if our existence is based in fear. We fear losing our parents, children, spouses, siblings, friends, pets.... The list goes on and on. But what is death, really?

I've been on a spiritual quest for years and the death of my husband only increased my seeking to know...where is he? Is he OK? Is he alive? I've written scenes in novels about the reality of everlasting life but still...this was MY husband!

Not a character in a fiction book.

Great spiritual leaders tell us that death is the door to life, a "crossing over" from the natural world back into the spiritual place from whence we all originated. Many say relationships don't end, they simply change form.

Most of us wonder and question, even seek mediums and others more "in tune" with the spiritual realm than we are—because we want to be assured what we believe is true. What we don't realize is those loved ones who've crossed from this life into the next often have ways of answering those questions for us. A dream, a vision, hearing their voice, or even actual visitation after their departure is often discounted as part of the grieving process instead of acknowledged as the miracle of blessed assurance it is!

Does this knowledge make you miss your loved one less?

Of course not! Being steeped in the physical realm, we will naturally long for and grieve the physical presence that is no longer there. However, knowing this will bring peace.

Eventually.

So let your soul live. Give it life by inviting the Spirit of the Lord to fill it. Seek Him, follow Him. You will be complete and content when your soul is in communion with its Savior and you will no longer fear death of the body but understand it is merely a transition.

***Seeds to Ponder:*** Whenever you close your eyes and feel a need for "more," ask yourself, is this a soul-deep need or is it the mindless chatter of your flesh (or ego) craving more so that you will feel better about yourself and/or those around you and the world in general will accept you or think more highly of you? Realize the difference. A soul-deep need can only be fulfilled by communion with God and should be reflective of His nature to love and give good things to others and to the world at large. A fleshly need is usually shallow and based in the material world.

**Prayer:** Lord God, help me discern the difference between the desires of my heart which lead to life and love and the mindless chatter of the flesh which quenches the spirit and leads to the hardening and death of my soul.

### *Reflection*

_____

_____

_____

Love is a Rose

## *Reflection*

Thibodeaux

## *Reflection*

Love is a Rose

***When the night has been too lonely,
and the road has been too long...***

When you've reached the end of your rope and you think that you can go no more, remember it is at these times He carries you! Cling to Him. Ask for His Holy Spirit to come closer to you. Jesus said, "I am going but I will not leave you alone. I will send you a comforter, a counselor to guide and help you."

I can't tell you how many times in my life I never thought I'd get through, yet somehow, by the grace of God, I managed.

The year was 2004. An auto accident created for me what the doctor termed, "situation induced depression." Many were the nights I'd go to sleep holding a cross in my hand and praying, "Lord, I can make it through the day but You're going to have to get me through the night." Though not the first, this was possibly the toughest year I'd faced in my life.

Until 2009.

That year started out unlike any I'd experienced. My husband, who'd suffered heart failure in 2005, woke up one day in excruciating pain. Weeks of trips to the emergency room finally ended with the discovery of non-Hodgkin's lymphoma. The easiest to cure with the best success rate of non-reoccurrence. *For otherwise healthy individuals.* Still we set out on our course with faith and optimism. He beat the cancer! But the strain and damaging side effects of chemotherapy was too much for his weakened heart to bear. My beloved had a massive heart attack and died on August 18th.

This journey through grief has been a road too long with many lonely nights, but on those days when all I could pray was, "I don't understand but I trust you," God pulled me through my darkest hour.

Whatever the situation, whatever the circumstance, He will carry you through, too! Seek Him, speak to Him, and cling to Him.

You can do this through prayer or meditation. Another effective means is simply by talking to Him. Tell Him your fears and concerns. He knows and understands. After all, He became man so that He could identify with our strengths, weaknesses and temptations. He suffered for us so He can suffer with us and carry us through our trials.

***Seeds to Ponder:*** We all experience a dark night of the soul. Whether the parting of a loved one, loss of a marriage, or end of a job we relished. Have you allowed this trial to darken your life or open your spirit to new possibilities?

**Prayer:** Dear God, take this experience which has darkened my life and turn it into a miracle for me and a lesson I can share in light and love that may bless others and make the world a kinder, more loving place.

## *Reflection*

_____

_____

_____

_____

_____

## *Reflection*

## Love is a Rose

***And you think that love is only for the lucky and the strong...***

**Remember:** *God is Love.* He gave His only son Jesus, and He died for you. He doesn't care how strong or how lucky you are. We are only lucky that He loved us enough to die for us and thereby reconcile us with the Father.

What is love, honestly? We hear songs, read books, listen to poetry and have this fairytale idea that love is a story book ending of happy-ever-after. Hey, I believe this too!

**Bottom line is; *love is a choice.***

Love makes the decision to stay when things get tough. Love chooses to be faithful when temptation to stray is everywhere. Love seeks peace and forgiveness when every fiber of your being is screaming for vindication and revenge. Love chooses to turn the other cheek, walk a mile in your brother's shoes, bless and pray for your enemies, stop murmuring, gossiping, complaining, and most of all—judging!

Love is laughter, joy, peace, gratitude, and bliss—and holds fast to patience, kindness and truth when the world around you is falling apart.

So when you're tempted to "throw in the towel" and you think that no one loves you or you're not strong enough or lucky enough or deserving of love, look to Jesus. Behold Him. Trust Him. Become more like Him and God will take care of the rest.

***Seeds to Ponder:*** In what way (by rejection or disappointment) and by whom has your heart been hardened so much that you doubt you'll ever find true love? Has this hardness protected you or has it closed you off to the possibility of miracles?

**Prayer:** God of Love, Your word says that he who dwells in love, dwells in You (John 4:16). Please take away this stony heart filled with anger and bitterness and give me a heart of love and forgiveness that I may offer love and forgiveness to a hurting world.

## *Reflection*

## *Reflection*

Love is a Rose

## *Just remember in the winter (of darkness or sin)....*

Sin is defined as anything that separates you from God. Sin causes you to think more highly of yourself than others.

Jesus died so that we might have life. He conquered sin and darkness, so why do we insist on living in these devastating attributes? Why do we allow the darkness and sin of others to permeate our souls so much that we become entrenched in the ways of the world instead of the ways of the Spirit?

As we reflect on our past, we can all recall times when our life was seeped in darkness. Depression, sin, (ours or those against us), financial stress, and emotional strain all create voids in our lives and emptiness in our souls. Many times these circumstances cause us to turn away from God.

Even if it is a slight shift, we feel it and HE knows it.

Some folks realize this right away and return to Him. Others live in their pit for years before enlightenment comes. Some never recover. God have mercy on us all and help us to remember that we are more than conquerors through Christ.

**Understand this:** The (Holy) Spirit of the living God dwells in you! By the power and revelation knowledge of His love acting and working in and through you, this world can become a heavenly place of love, light, peace and joy.

*Seeds to Ponder*: Spiritually we are all connected. In what way and in how many areas of your life have you allowed the darkness of pain or bitterness caused by anger, hatred, or prejudice to separate you from God and from your fellow man?

**Prayer:** Heavenly Father, eradicate darkness and sin from my life that I may be a joy to You and a blessing unto this world.

*Reflection*

_____

_____

## *Reflection*

## *Reflection*

Love is a Rose

***Far beneath the bitter snows...***

How can something so beautiful and pure, be so bitter and cold? God is light. He washes us clean with the shed blood of His son so that we might be as pure as the snow. As treacherous and dangerous as they may be, snow flurries and ice storms produce beautiful prisms of light and beauty. Remember, God is in the winter of our lives, just as He is in the winter of nature and there is a purpose for every moment of your life.

I doubt anyone wakes up on a given day and decides to be a negative, bitter person. We are not born to harbor resentment and seek vengeance. Look at babies and little children! I remember so many times while growing up my brothers or I would have a quarrel or disagreement with one of our neighbors. Mama would always say adults should not interfere in these disputes unless they turn toward violence that might cause bodily injury.

Jesus taught us to become as little children because children know (and practice) the art of letting go and forgiving

—which most adults have forgotten. Most of the time, the kids will be over the little hurdle and playing again while the adults are still fighting!

Now granted a person can only take so much abuse before it takes its toll. If that is your case, remember one thing....You may have a very valid reason for being the way you are, but there is no excuse to stay that way!

The law of attraction states, "*What you focus on, you attract.*" The Bible says, "*As a man thinks he is*" and "*you reap what you sow.*"

If your life is filled with negative circumstances, examine your heart, your thoughts, your words and your actions and see if you are sowing negative seeds and reaping a harvest worthy of what you've sown.

How do you let go, forgive, change your life?

By changing your thoughts and words. Begin with forgiving everyone you hold a grievance against and forgive yourself for the years you allowed their actions to dictate your life. Even if you don't 'feel' like its working, keep doing this until you have been set free and watch your life blossom into a beautiful garden of grace!

***Seeds to Ponder:*** What experience(s) in your life have caused you a hardness of heart or coldness of spirit?

**Prayer:** Father God, fill the cold, bitter places in my heart with Your love and light that I, in turn, my be a vessel of love and light in this world.

### *Reflection*

_____

_____

_____

_____

_____

_____

_____

*Reflection*

## Love is a Rose

***Lies the seed*** (of faith)...
***that with the sun's*** (Son's) ***love...***
***in the spring...*** (season of new birth, new life)
***...becomes the rose*** (an attractive flower).

Jesus said that if we have faith the size of the mustard seed we could move mountains. He also told of the mustard tree which, although born of the tiniest of seeds, becomes a huge tree able to house and feed birds. The Bible states that when we accept Jesus as our Lord, we are born again, "not of corruptible seed but of incorruptible seed." (1 Peter 1:23).

What does this mean?

It means that the seed of God (Love) is buried deep in our hearts and as we nurture (water) that seed (with the truth of God's promises in the light of His love for us) it is able to produce a harvest of love and goodness in our lives and in the lives of others.

How can one accomplish this when there is so much darkness, coldness, and callousness of heart all around?

Simple.

I John 4:16 states. "God is love and he who dwells in love, dwells in God and God in him."

Sit quietly, close your eyes, breathe deep and repeat the phrase, "I love you." Just say the words and allow the love residing deep in your heart to rise up. Eventually those words produce a harvest of others.... Thank you...I forgive you....Bless you....Peace be with you...

Practice this and soon you will find that you are surrounding every person and circumstance in your life with love and love will permeate your every thought, word and action.

In those moments you become more like God.

**Seeds to ponder**: What seeds are you planting in your life and the lives of others? Seeds of love, peace, joy, forgiveness, and abundance...or seeds of anger, hatred, bitterness, and lack?

Love is a Rose

**Prayer:** Holy Father, dig up the seeds of negativism in my heart and eradicate darkness from my mind so that the light and love of your Spirit may rise within me to shower Your love and goodness onto the world.

## *Reflection*

## *Reflection*

Love is a Rose

***Dearest Reader,***

With God's love, mercy, and forgiveness, even the ugliest sinner can become as pure as snow, as attractive as a flower. We are called to "live in the light."

Jesus said, "I am the light of the world."

We are to let "the light of Christ" shine through us and brighten our world; a world darkened by sin.

I am calling you to become a rose...an attractive flower in the jungle of life.

It is my most sincere prayer, that this analogy will bring you peace, joy and blessings as you apply the wisdom of words to your own spiritual journey.

Remember: "With God all things are possible" and "nothing is impossible to him that believes."


God Bless You.
Pamela S Thibodeaux
***"Inspirational with an Edge!"*** ™

## *Reflection*

## *Reflection*

## *Reflection*

## *Reflection*

## *Reflection*

Love is a Rose

## *Reflection*

## *Reflection*

## *About the Author*

Award-winning author, Pamela S. Thibodeaux is the Co-Founder and a lifetime member of Bayou Writers Group in Lake Charles, Louisiana and the Owner/CEO of The Wordsmith Journal Magazine.

Pamela grew up in the town of Iowa, Louisiana. She is a mother, grandmother and deeply committed Christian who firmly believes in God and His promises.

*"God is very real to me and I feel that people today need and want to hear more of His truths wherever they can glean them. People are hungry for practical (and real) Christian values, not some 'holier-than-thou' beliefs that are impossible to believe and impossible to live up to,"* Pamela says.

*"I do my best to encourage readers to develop a personal relationship with God. The deepest desire of my heart is to glorify God and to get His message of faith, trust and forgiveness to a hurting world."*

Multi-published in romantic fiction as well as creative non-fiction, her writing has been tagged as**, "Inspirational with an Edge!"** ™ and reviewed as *"steamier and grittier than the typical Christian novel without decreasing the message."*

Find out more about Pamela by visiting her website and/or blog and connect with her on FaceBook, Twitter @psthib or LinkedIn.

## *Other Titles by Pamela S Thibodeaux*

Lori Strickland (introduced in ***Tempered Fire***) has always been known as her father's "wild child" with no desire to change until she meets ex-bull-rider-turned-preacher Rafe Judson. Her attempts to change her wanton ways come to naught until she realizes redemption only comes with true repentance. Can she find redemption and win the heart of the cowboy preacher? Find out in ***Lori's Redemption***

A visionary is someone who sees into the future Taylor Forrestier sees into the past but only as it pertains to her work. Hailed by her peers as "a visionary with an instinct for beauty and an eye for the unique" Taylor is undoubtedly a brilliant architect and gifted designer. But she and twin brother Trevor, share more than a successful business. The two share a childhood wrought with lies and deceit and the kind of abuse that's disgustingly prevalent in today's society. Can the love of God and the awesome healing power of His grace and mercy free the twins from their past and open their hearts to the good plan and the future He has for their lives? Find out in ***The Visionary*** ~ *Where the awesome power of God's love heals the most wounded of souls.*

***The Inheritance*** is about the chance we all long for...the chance to start over...

Widowed at age thirty-nine and suffering from empty nest syndrome, Rebecca Sinclair is overshadowed by grief and loneliness. Her husband has been deceased for a year, her oldest child has moved to New York in pursuit of an acting career and her youngest child is attending college in France. Having spent over half of her life as a wife and mother, she has no idea what God has in store for her now. Will an unexpected inheritance in the wine country of New York bring meaning and purpose to her life and give her the courage to love again?

US Postal worker Raymond Jacobey has been in love with the little widow since he first set eyes on her. A wanderer searching for the ever-illusive soul mate, Ray has never stayed in one place too long. Raised by self-centered, high-power executives, he's longed for the idyllic life of residing in a cozy house in a small town with the love of his life. Will he gain the heart of the lovely widow or will he lose her to the wine country of New York?    Find out in ***The Inheritance***

Single mom Cathy Johnson is tired of running her life alone...what she needs is a well-trained angel to help out. Jared Savoy gave up the dream of having a family when he discovered he is sterile. Can a confirmed bachelor and the mother of four find love amid normal daily chaos? Find out in ***Cathy's Angel***

Best-selling novelist and songwriter, Camie Rogers has penned numerous accounts of the secret love she holds in her heart. Country-Music Superstar Kip Allen has changed from the shy, humble boy, to the epitome of "star." Can the two rediscover each other after one night of his Home is Where the Heart is Tour? Find out in ***Choices***

Anthony Paul Seville is known as the 'most eligible bachelor' in New Orleans, possibly even the entire state of Louisiana, but finds himself alone—completely and explicitly alone. Jessica Aucoin is a writer on her way to fame and fortune, but is haunted by a man from her past. Will the "champion" lawyer and the author of romantic suspense find love written in their future? Find out in ***A Hero for Jessica***

Sienna has survived what most succumb to - the death of a spouse and child and has maintained her faith despite her troubles. William has never met anyone who actually lived out what they say they believe. Is it true love between the faithful optimist and broody pessimist or simply ***Winter Madness?***

Grade school teacher Carson Alexander has a gift—a gift that has driven a wedge between him and his family. Worse, it's put him at odds with God. Feeling alone and misunderstood, Carson views God's gift of prophecy as the worst kind of curse...that is until he meets Lorelei Conner, landscape artist extraordinaire, and perhaps the one person who may need Carson and his gift more than anyone ever has. Lorelei Connor is a mother on the run. Her abusive ex-husband has followed her all over the country trying to steal their daughter. Distrusting of men and needing to keep on the move, she's surprised by her desire to remain close to Carson Alexander. Through her fear and hesitation, she must learn to rely on God to guide her—not an easy task when He's prompting her to trust a man. Can their relationship withstand the tragedy lurking on the horizon? Find out ***in In His Sight***

Jason Stockwell has been commissioned to interview Kylie Erickson and to review her books. Only problem is, she won't give the time of day much less an interview to someone whose type of writing she deems not worthy of respect. Can they suspend their judgmental attitudes and find true love? Find out ***in Review of Love*** (A FREE read from Pelican Book Group/White Rose Publishing!)

***Tempered Hearts:*** Rancher Craig Harris and veterinarian Tamera Collins clash from the moment they meet. Innocence is pitted against arrogance as tempers rise and passions ignite to form a love as pure as the finest gold, fresh from the crucible and as strong as steel. Thrown together amid tragedy and unsated passion, Tamera and Craig share a strong attraction that neither accepts as the first stages of love. Torn between desire and dislike, they must make peace with their pasts and God in order to open up to the love blossoming between them. It is a love that nothing can destroy when they come to understand that *only when hearts are tempered, minds are opened and wills are softened can man discern the will of God for his life.*

Dr. Scott Hensley (introduced in *Tempered Hearts*) has built a wall around his heart since the death of his wife and parents. Katrina Simmons is recovering from scars inflicted on her as a battered wife. Can dreams be renewed and faith strengthened? Can they find joy and peace in God's love and in love for one another? Find out in **Tempered Dreams**

Amber Harris is a good girl on the brink of womanhood. Stanley Morrison is a young man at the start of his life. For each other, they have always felt the fireworks that two people in love should feel. But the questions about his past, his pride, and Amber's father might be the end of what could be a strong relationship. As the two try to protect their budding romance, some unlikely but powerful forces conspire to keep them apart. Will they survive the wishes of everyone around them with their relationship intact? Find out in ***Tempered Fire***

All around rodeo cowboy and heir to the Rockin' H Ranch, Ace Harris is determined not to fall in love. He's only loved one woman in his life, his mother, and no one can even come close to filling her boots. Lexie Morgan thinks rodeo cowboys have rocks for brains and a death wish for a soul. A broken childhood and the death of her father and best friend leave her doubting and questioning God (despite her years of religious upbringing) and afraid of love. Can two young people who clash from the onset learn to trust in the healing power of God and find love and happiness amidst tragedy and grief? Find out in ***Tempered Joy***

*Temperance*

*Publishing*

www.ingramcontent.com/pod-product-compliance
Lightning Source LLC
Chambersburg PA
CBHW072059290426
44110CB00014B/1753